50 Premium Beef Recipes for the House

By: Kelly Johnson

Table of Contents

- Beef Wellington
- Ribeye Steak with Herb Butter
- Braised Short Ribs
- Prime Rib Roast
- Filet Mignon with Red Wine Reduction
- Beef Stroganoff
- Korean BBQ Beef (Bulgogi)
- Beef Bourguignon
- Grilled Tomahawk Steak
- Shabu-Shabu
- Teriyaki Beef Skewers
- Slow-Cooked Brisket
- Wagyu Steak with Sea Salt
- Thai Beef Salad
- Steak Tartare
- Argentine Chimichurri Steak
- Beef Kofta Kebabs

- Vietnamese Pho with Rare Beef
- Garlic Butter Skillet Steak Bites
- Coffee-Rubbed Sirloin
- Spicy Mongolian Beef
- Red Wine Braised Chuck Roast
- Texas-Style Smoked Brisket
- Beef and Broccoli Stir-Fry
- Steak au Poivre
- Mediterranean Beef Kabobs
- Slow-Cooked Osso Buco
- Japanese Gyudon
- Jamaican Jerk Beef
- Horseradish Crusted Prime Rib
- Moroccan Spiced Beef Tagine
- Classic Roast Beef
- Grilled Flank Steak with Chimichurri
- Cuban Ropa Vieja
- Stuffed Bell Peppers with Beef
- French Dip Sandwich

- Guinness Braised Beef
- Korean Galbi (Short Ribs)
- Surf and Turf
- Beef Empanadas
- Braised Oxtail
- Grilled Beef Tenderloin Medallions
- Philly Cheesesteak
- Japanese Sukiyaki
- Cajun Blackened Ribeye
- Brazilian Picanha
- Ground Beef Wellington Cups
- Swedish Meatballs
- Butter Garlic Beef Ribs
- Cuban Mojo Marinated Steak

Beef Wellington

Ingredients:

- 2 lb beef tenderloin (center-cut)
- Salt and pepper
- 2 tbsp olive oil
- 2 tbsp Dijon mustard
- 8 oz mushrooms, finely chopped
- 2 tbsp butter
- 2 shallots, minced
- 2 cloves garlic, minced
- 6–8 slices prosciutto
- 1 sheet puff pastry, thawed
- 1 egg, beaten

Instructions:

1. Sear the tenderloin on all sides in olive oil, about 2 minutes per side. Let cool. Brush with Dijon mustard.
2. Sauté shallots, garlic, and mushrooms in butter until moisture evaporates. Cool.
3. Lay prosciutto on plastic wrap, spread mushroom mixture on top, place beef in the center. Roll tightly and chill 15 mins.
4. Roll out puff pastry, wrap the beef roll in it. Chill again.

5. Brush with egg wash. Bake at 425°F (220°C) for 35–40 mins. Rest before slicing.

Ribeye Steak with Herb Butter

Ingredients:

- 2 ribeye steaks
- Salt and pepper
- 2 tbsp oil
- 2 tbsp butter
- 2 garlic cloves, smashed
- 2 sprigs rosemary or thyme

Herb Butter:

- 1/4 cup butter, softened
- 1 tsp chopped parsley
- 1 tsp chopped thyme
- Salt and pepper

Instructions:

1. Mix herb butter and chill.
2. Season steaks. Sear in hot oil, 3–4 mins per side.
3. Add butter, garlic, herbs; baste for 1–2 mins.
4. Rest steaks 5 mins, top with herb butter.

Braised Short Ribs

Ingredients:

- 4 lbs bone-in beef short ribs
- Salt, pepper, flour (for dusting)
- 2 tbsp oil
- 1 onion, chopped
- 2 carrots, chopped
- 2 celery stalks, chopped
- 3 cloves garlic, minced
- 2 tbsp tomato paste
- 2 cups red wine
- 2 cups beef broth
- 2 sprigs thyme

Instructions:

1. Season and sear ribs. Remove and set aside.
2. Sauté onion, carrot, celery. Add garlic, tomato paste.
3. Deglaze with wine, add broth and thyme.
4. Return ribs to pot, cover and braise at 325°F (160°C) for 2.5–3 hrs.
5. Skim fat, reduce sauce if desired.

Prime Rib Roast

Ingredients:

- 5 lb prime rib roast
- 3 tbsp olive oil
- 1 tbsp salt
- 1 tbsp pepper
- 1 tbsp garlic powder
- 1 tbsp rosemary

Instructions:

1. Let roast come to room temp. Preheat oven to 450°F (230°C).
2. Rub with oil and seasonings.
3. Roast 20 minutes, then reduce to 325°F (165°C) and cook to desired doneness (about 15 mins/lb for medium rare).
4. Rest 20–30 mins before slicing.

Filet Mignon with Red Wine Reduction

Ingredients:

- 4 filet mignon steaks
- Salt, pepper
- 2 tbsp oil
- 1 tbsp butter

Red Wine Sauce:

- 1 cup red wine
- 1/2 cup beef broth
- 1 shallot, minced
- 1 tbsp butter

Instructions:

1. Sear steaks in oil until desired doneness. Rest.
2. Sauté shallot, deglaze with wine, add broth. Reduce by half.
3. Finish with butter. Spoon over steaks.

Beef Stroganoff

Ingredients:

- 1 lb beef sirloin, thinly sliced
- Salt, pepper, flour
- 2 tbsp oil
- 1 onion, chopped
- 8 oz mushrooms, sliced
- 1 tbsp Dijon mustard
- 1 cup beef broth
- 1/2 cup sour cream
- Egg noodles

Instructions:

1. Dust beef with flour. Sear and set aside.
2. Sauté onion and mushrooms. Add broth and mustard. Simmer.
3. Return beef, then stir in sour cream.
4. Serve over noodles.

Korean BBQ Beef (Bulgogi)

Ingredients:

- 1 lb thinly sliced beef ribeye
- 1/4 cup soy sauce
- 2 tbsp brown sugar
- 1 tbsp sesame oil
- 1 tbsp mirin
- 2 garlic cloves, minced
- 1 tsp grated ginger
- 1/2 pear, grated
- 1/4 tsp black pepper
- Green onion, sesame seeds

Instructions:

1. Mix marinade, add beef. Marinate at least 30 mins.
2. Grill or pan-fry until caramelized.
3. Garnish with sesame seeds and green onion.

Beef Bourguignon

Ingredients:

- 2.5 lbs beef chuck, cubed
- Salt, pepper, flour
- 2 tbsp oil
- 1 onion, chopped
- 2 carrots, chopped
- 3 cloves garlic
- 2 tbsp tomato paste
- 2 cups red wine
- 2 cups beef broth
- 1 bay leaf, thyme
- 8 oz mushrooms
- 8 pearl onions

Instructions:

1. Brown beef in batches, set aside.
2. Sauté onions, carrots, garlic. Add tomato paste.
3. Add wine, broth, herbs, beef. Simmer 2 hours.
4. Sauté mushrooms and pearl onions separately, stir in before serving.

Grilled Tomahawk Steak

Ingredients:

- 1 tomahawk ribeye steak (2–3 lbs)
- Salt and freshly ground black pepper
- 2 tbsp olive oil
- 2 cloves garlic, smashed
- 2 sprigs rosemary or thyme

Instructions:

1. Let steak come to room temp. Rub with oil, salt, and pepper.
2. Sear over high heat (3–4 mins/side), then finish on indirect heat until internal temp reaches 125°F (52°C) for medium-rare.
3. During last minutes, baste with garlic and rosemary-infused butter.
4. Rest 10–15 minutes before slicing.

Shabu-Shabu

Ingredients:

- 1 lb thinly sliced beef (ribeye or sirloin)
- Napa cabbage, mushrooms, tofu, carrots, udon noodles
- Kombu dashi broth

Dipping Sauces:

- Ponzu sauce
- Sesame sauce

Instructions:

1. Simmer kombu in water (remove before boiling). Add vegetables and cook until tender.
2. Swish beef slices in the broth for a few seconds until just cooked.
3. Dip in sauces and serve with rice.

Teriyaki Beef Skewers

Ingredients:

- 1 lb sirloin steak, cubed
- 1/4 cup soy sauce
- 2 tbsp mirin
- 2 tbsp sake
- 1 tbsp sugar
- Garlic and ginger (optional)

Instructions:

1. Combine marinade ingredients. Marinate beef for 1–2 hours.
2. Thread beef onto skewers. Grill or broil, basting with marinade, until caramelized and cooked through.

Slow-Cooked Brisket

Ingredients:

- 3–4 lb beef brisket
- 1 onion, sliced
- 4 cloves garlic, smashed
- 1 cup beef broth
- 1/2 cup red wine (optional)
- 1/4 cup tomato paste or BBQ sauce
- Salt, pepper, paprika

Instructions:

1. Season brisket. Sear both sides in a skillet.
2. Place in slow cooker with onion, garlic, broth, and tomato paste.
3. Cook on low for 8–10 hours. Slice or shred and serve.

Wagyu Steak with Sea Salt

Ingredients:

- 1 Wagyu steak (ribeye or striploin)
- Coarse sea salt
- Freshly ground pepper

Instructions:

1. Let steak reach room temp. Season lightly with salt and pepper.
2. Sear in hot dry pan (or cast iron) 1–2 mins per side (depends on thickness).
3. Rest briefly, slice thinly, serve as-is or with wasabi and soy.

Thai Beef Salad (Yam Nua)

Ingredients:

- 8 oz grilled sirloin, thinly sliced
- Mixed greens, cucumber, cherry tomatoes, red onion
- Fresh mint, cilantro

Dressing:

- 2 tbsp lime juice
- 1 tbsp fish sauce
- 1 tsp sugar
- 1 chili, minced

Instructions:

1. Grill steak, rest, and slice.
2. Toss salad ingredients.
3. Combine dressing, pour over, and toss gently.

Steak Tartare

Ingredients:

- 6 oz raw beef tenderloin, finely chopped
- 1 tsp Dijon mustard
- 1 tsp capers, chopped
- 1 tsp shallots, minced
- 1 egg yolk
- Worcestershire sauce, hot sauce
- Salt, pepper

Instructions:

1. Mix beef with mustard, capers, shallots, and seasonings.
2. Shape into a mound, top with egg yolk. Serve with toast or crackers.

Argentine Chimichurri Steak

Ingredients:

- 2 lb flank or skirt steak
- Salt and pepper

Chimichurri Sauce:

- 1 cup parsley, chopped
- 2 tbsp oregano
- 2 garlic cloves, minced
- 1/2 cup olive oil
- 2 tbsp red wine vinegar
- 1/2 tsp red pepper flakes

Instructions:

1. Mix chimichurri ingredients. Let sit for 15 mins.
2. Grill steak to desired doneness. Rest and slice.
3. Spoon chimichurri on top.

Beef Kofta Kebabs

Ingredients:

- 1 lb ground beef
- 1/2 onion, grated
- 2 garlic cloves, minced
- 2 tbsp parsley, chopped
- 1 tsp cumin
- 1 tsp coriander
- 1/2 tsp cinnamon
- Salt and pepper

Instructions:

1. Mix all ingredients. Shape into logs on skewers.
2. Grill or broil for 8–10 mins, turning to brown all sides.
3. Serve with tzatziki and flatbread.

Vietnamese Pho with Rare Beef

Broth Ingredients:

- 1 onion, halved
- 1 3-inch piece ginger, halved
- 3–4 lbs beef bones (marrow and knuckle)
- 2 cinnamon sticks, 3 star anise, 1 tbsp coriander seeds
- 1 tbsp fish sauce
- Salt to taste

To Serve:

- Thinly sliced raw beef (sirloin or eye of round)
- Cooked rice noodles
- Bean sprouts, lime, herbs (basil, cilantro), chili

Instructions:

1. Char onion and ginger. Simmer with bones and spices for 6–8 hrs. Strain and season.
2. Assemble bowl with noodles, raw beef, and toppings. Pour boiling broth over beef to cook.

Garlic Butter Skillet Steak Bites

Ingredients:

- 1 lb sirloin, cut into 1-inch cubes
- 3 tbsp butter
- 4 garlic cloves, minced
- Salt, pepper, parsley

Instructions:

1. Season steak cubes. Sear in a hot skillet 2–3 mins until browned.
2. Lower heat, add butter and garlic. Cook 1 more min, tossing to coat.
3. Garnish with parsley and serve.

Coffee-Rubbed Sirloin

Ingredients:

- 1 sirloin steak (1.5 lbs)
- 1 tbsp finely ground coffee
- 1 tbsp brown sugar
- 1 tsp smoked paprika
- Salt and pepper

Instructions:

1. Combine rub ingredients. Pat onto steak.
2. Grill or pan-sear to desired doneness. Rest and slice.

Spicy Mongolian Beef

Ingredients:

- 1 lb flank steak, sliced thin
- 1/4 cup cornstarch
- 1/4 cup soy sauce
- 1/4 cup brown sugar
- 1/2 cup water
- 2 garlic cloves, minced
- 1 tsp ginger, minced
- Red chili flakes
- Green onions

Instructions:

1. Toss beef in cornstarch. Sear in hot oil.
2. Remove, then sauté garlic and ginger. Add soy sauce, sugar, water. Simmer.
3. Return beef, coat in sauce, top with chili flakes and green onions.

Red Wine Braised Chuck Roast

Ingredients:

- 3 lb chuck roast
- Salt, pepper
- 2 tbsp tomato paste
- 1 onion, 3 carrots, 2 celery stalks, chopped
- 2 cups red wine
- 2 cups beef broth
- 3 garlic cloves, thyme, bay leaf

Instructions:

1. Brown roast. Remove, sauté veggies and tomato paste.
2. Deglaze with wine, add broth and herbs. Return beef.
3. Braise covered at 325°F (163°C) for 3 hours until tender.

Texas-Style Smoked Brisket

Ingredients:

- 5–8 lb beef brisket
- Mustard (binder)
- Rub: equal parts salt and black pepper

Instructions:

1. Coat brisket in mustard, apply rub liberally.
2. Smoke at 225°F (107°C) for 12–14 hours until 195–203°F (90–95°C) internal temp.
3. Rest for 1 hour, slice against the grain.

Beef and Broccoli Stir-Fry

Ingredients:

- 1 lb flank steak, thinly sliced
- 2 cups broccoli florets
- 2 tbsp soy sauce
- 2 tbsp oyster sauce
- 1 tbsp cornstarch
- 1 tsp sesame oil
- 2 garlic cloves, minced

Instructions:

1. Marinate beef in soy, cornstarch, sesame oil.
2. Stir-fry beef in hot oil. Remove.
3. Cook broccoli, add garlic, sauces, and return beef. Stir to coat and serve over rice.

Steak au Poivre

Ingredients:

- 2 filet mignon steaks
- 2 tbsp black peppercorns, crushed
- Salt
- 2 tbsp butter
- 1/4 cup cognac or brandy
- 1/2 cup heavy cream

Instructions:

1. Press peppercorns into steaks. Season with salt.
2. Sear steaks in butter, 3–4 minutes per side for medium-rare. Remove.
3. Deglaze pan with cognac, then add cream. Simmer until thickened.
4. Serve sauce over steaks.

Mediterranean Beef Kabobs

Ingredients:

- 1 lb beef sirloin, cubed
- 1 red onion, 1 bell pepper, 1 zucchini, all cut into chunks
- Marinade: 1/4 cup olive oil, 2 tbsp lemon juice, 2 garlic cloves, oregano, salt, pepper

Instructions:

1. Marinate beef and veggies 1 hour.
2. Thread onto skewers.
3. Grill 8–10 minutes, turning, until beef is cooked through.

Slow-Cooked Osso Buco

Ingredients:

- 4 beef shanks
- Salt, pepper, flour for dredging
- 2 tbsp olive oil
- 1 onion, 2 carrots, 2 celery stalks, diced
- 1 cup red wine
- 2 cups beef broth
- 1 tbsp tomato paste
- 2 garlic cloves, thyme, bay leaf

Instructions:

1. Season and dredge shanks. Brown in oil. Remove.
2. Sauté vegetables, add tomato paste. Deglaze with wine.
3. Add broth and herbs. Return shanks, cover and simmer for 3–4 hours until tender.

Japanese Gyudon (Beef Bowl)

Ingredients:

- 1 lb thinly sliced beef (ribeye or chuck)
- 1 onion, sliced
- Sauce: 1/2 cup dashi, 1/4 cup soy sauce, 1/4 cup mirin, 1 tbsp sugar

Instructions:

1. Simmer onion in sauce until soft.
2. Add beef, cook until no longer pink.
3. Serve over steamed rice, garnish with pickled ginger and green onions.

Jamaican Jerk Beef

Ingredients:

- 1 lb flank steak

- Jerk marinade: 2 scallions, 1 scotch bonnet pepper, 1 tsp allspice, 1 tsp thyme, 1 tbsp soy sauce, 1 tbsp vinegar, garlic, ginger

Instructions:

1. Blend marinade. Rub into steak and marinate overnight.

2. Grill or pan-sear to desired doneness.

3. Slice and serve with rice and peas.

Horseradish Crusted Prime Rib

Ingredients:

- 4–5 lb prime rib roast

- Crust: 1/4 cup horseradish, 1/4 cup breadcrumbs, 2 tbsp olive oil, garlic, rosemary, salt, pepper

Instructions:

1. Pat roast dry. Coat with horseradish crust.

2. Roast at 450°F (230°C) for 20 mins, then at 325°F (163°C) until 125°F (52°C) internal temp (medium-rare).

3. Rest before slicing.

Moroccan Spiced Beef Tagine

Ingredients:

- 2 lbs beef stew meat
- 1 onion, chopped
- 2 garlic cloves, minced
- Spices: cumin, coriander, cinnamon, paprika, turmeric
- 1 can diced tomatoes
- 1/2 cup beef broth
- 1/2 cup dried apricots or prunes
- Chickpeas (optional)

Instructions:

1. Brown beef. Remove.
2. Sauté onion and garlic, add spices.
3. Return beef with tomatoes, broth, and fruit. Simmer for 2 hours until tender.
4. Serve with couscous.

Classic Roast Beef

Ingredients:

- 3–4 lb top round roast
- Salt, pepper, garlic powder, rosemary
- Olive oil

Instructions:

1. Rub roast with oil and seasonings.
2. Roast at 450°F (230°C) for 15 mins, reduce to 325°F (163°C) and roast until 130°F (54°C) internal temp.
3. Rest, slice thin, and serve with jus or gravy.

Grilled Flank Steak with Chimichurri

Ingredients:

- 1.5 lbs flank steak
- Salt and pepper

Chimichurri Sauce:

- 1 cup parsley
- 3 garlic cloves
- 2 tbsp red wine vinegar
- 1/2 cup olive oil
- 1 tsp oregano
- 1/2 tsp red pepper flakes
- Salt to taste

Instructions:

1. Blend chimichurri ingredients. Let sit.
2. Season steak with salt and pepper. Grill 4–5 mins per side.
3. Rest, slice thinly, and spoon chimichurri on top.

Cuban Ropa Vieja

Ingredients:

- 2 lbs flank steak
- 1 onion, 1 bell pepper, sliced
- 3 garlic cloves
- 1 can crushed tomatoes
- 1/2 cup beef broth
- 1 tsp cumin, 1 tsp oregano, 1 bay leaf
- Salt and pepper

Instructions:

1. Cook steak in a slow cooker with all ingredients for 6–8 hrs.
2. Shred meat and return to sauce.
3. Serve with rice and black beans.

Stuffed Bell Peppers with Beef

Ingredients:

- 4 bell peppers, tops cut, seeds removed
- 1 lb ground beef
- 1 cup cooked rice
- 1/2 onion, diced
- 1 cup tomato sauce
- 1 tsp garlic powder, salt, pepper
- 1/2 cup shredded cheese

Instructions:

1. Brown beef and onion. Mix with rice, sauce, and seasonings.
2. Fill peppers, top with cheese.
3. Bake at 375°F (190°C) for 25–30 mins.

French Dip Sandwich

Ingredients:

- 1.5 lbs roast beef, thinly sliced
- 4 hoagie rolls
- 4 slices provolone cheese
- 2 cups beef broth
- 1 tbsp Worcestershire sauce
- 1 tsp garlic powder

Instructions:

1. Simmer broth with Worcestershire and garlic.
2. Warm beef in broth.
3. Assemble sandwiches with beef and cheese, toast until melted. Serve with broth for dipping.

Guinness Braised Beef

Ingredients:

- 2.5 lbs beef chuck, cubed
- 1 onion, 2 carrots, chopped
- 2 garlic cloves
- 1 can Guinness stout
- 2 cups beef broth
- 1 tbsp tomato paste
- Thyme, salt, pepper

Instructions:

1. Brown beef. Remove.
2. Sauté vegetables and garlic, add tomato paste.
3. Add beer, broth, and herbs. Simmer 2.5–3 hours.
4. Serve over mashed potatoes.

Korean Galbi (Short Ribs)

Ingredients:

- 2 lbs beef short ribs (flanken cut)
- Marinade: 1/2 cup soy sauce, 1/4 cup sugar, 2 tbsp sesame oil, 1 tbsp rice wine, garlic, ginger, scallions

Instructions:

1. Marinate ribs overnight.
2. Grill or pan-sear until cooked through and caramelized.
3. Serve with rice and kimchi.

Surf and Turf

Ingredients:

- 2 filet mignon steaks
- 2 lobster tails
- Salt, pepper, butter, garlic

Instructions:

1. Season steaks and grill or pan-sear to desired doneness.
2. Broil lobster tails with garlic butter until opaque (6–8 mins).
3. Serve together with more garlic butter.

Beef Empanadas

Ingredients:

- 1 lb ground beef
- 1/2 onion, diced
- 1/4 cup olives, chopped
- 1/4 cup raisins (optional)
- 1 tsp cumin, paprika
- Empanada dough rounds
- 1 egg (for wash)

Instructions:

1. Brown beef with onion and seasonings. Add olives and raisins. Cool.
2. Fill dough rounds, seal, and crimp edges.
3. Brush with egg wash. Bake at 375°F (190°C) for 20–25 mins.

Braised Oxtail

Ingredients:

- 2.5 lbs oxtail
- Salt, pepper, flour (for dredging)
- 2 tbsp olive oil
- 1 onion, 2 carrots, 2 celery stalks, chopped
- 4 garlic cloves
- 2 tbsp tomato paste
- 1 cup red wine
- 3 cups beef broth
- 2 sprigs thyme, 2 bay leaves

Instructions:

1. Season and dredge oxtail in flour. Brown in oil, set aside.
2. Sauté vegetables and garlic. Add tomato paste, cook 2 mins.
3. Add wine to deglaze. Return oxtail, add broth and herbs.
4. Braise at 325°F (160°C) for 3 hours. Serve with mashed potatoes or polenta.

Grilled Beef Tenderloin Medallions

Ingredients:

- 4 beef tenderloin medallions (6 oz each)
- Salt, pepper, olive oil
- 2 garlic cloves, minced
- Fresh rosemary or thyme (optional)

Instructions:

1. Rub steaks with oil, garlic, salt, pepper, and herbs.
2. Grill on high heat 3–4 mins per side for medium-rare.
3. Rest 5 mins before serving. Top with compound butter if desired.

Philly Cheesesteak

Ingredients:

- 1 lb ribeye, thinly sliced
- 1 green bell pepper, 1 onion, sliced
- 4 hoagie rolls
- 8 slices provolone cheese
- Salt, pepper, oil

Instructions:

1. Sauté onion and peppers until soft. Set aside.
2. Cook beef in batches, season.
3. Mix with veggies, layer cheese over top to melt.
4. Load into rolls. Toast if desired.

Japanese Sukiyaki

Ingredients:

- 1 lb thin-sliced beef (ribeye or sirloin)
- 1 block tofu, cubed
- Napa cabbage, shiitake mushrooms, green onions, sliced
- 2 packs shirataki noodles
- 1/4 cup soy sauce, 1/4 cup mirin, 2 tbsp sugar, 1/4 cup sake

Instructions:

1. Mix sauce ingredients.
2. In a hot pot or pan, sauté beef briefly, then add sauce.
3. Add veggies, tofu, and noodles. Simmer gently and serve hot.
4. Optional: Dip cooked items in raw egg (traditional method).

Cajun Blackened Ribeye

Ingredients:

- 2 ribeye steaks
- 2 tbsp Cajun seasoning
- 1 tbsp butter
- Salt

Instructions:

1. Rub steaks with Cajun seasoning.
2. Heat cast iron pan until smoking. Sear steaks 3–4 mins per side.
3. Add butter at end, baste. Rest and serve.

Brazilian Picanha

Ingredients:

- 2–3 lb picanha roast (top sirloin cap)
- Coarse sea salt

Instructions:

1. Cut meat into 3–4 thick steaks, leaving fat cap intact.
2. Skewer into a "C" shape (traditional style), season generously.
3. Grill over charcoal or high heat until medium-rare.
4. Rest and slice against the grain.

Ground Beef Wellington Cups

Ingredients:

- 1 lb ground beef
- 1 small onion, finely chopped
- 2 cloves garlic, minced
- 1 cup mushrooms, finely chopped
- 1 tbsp Worcestershire sauce
- Salt and pepper
- 1 sheet puff pastry, thawed
- 1 egg, beaten (for egg wash)

Instructions:

1. Preheat oven to 400°F (200°C).
2. Sauté onion, garlic, and mushrooms until soft. Add ground beef and cook until browned. Stir in Worcestershire sauce, salt, and pepper. Cool slightly.
3. Cut puff pastry into squares, press into a muffin tin.
4. Fill each cup with the beef mixture. Brush edges with egg wash.
5. Bake 15–20 minutes until pastry is golden. Serve warm.

Swedish Meatballs

Ingredients:

- 1 lb ground beef
- 1/2 cup breadcrumbs
- 1/4 cup milk
- 1 small onion, grated
- 1 egg
- 1/2 tsp nutmeg
- Salt and pepper

For the sauce:

- 2 tbsp butter
- 2 tbsp flour
- 2 cups beef broth
- 1/2 cup heavy cream
- 1 tsp Worcestershire sauce

Instructions:

1. Mix beef, breadcrumbs soaked in milk, onion, egg, nutmeg, salt, and pepper. Form into small meatballs.
2. Brown meatballs in a skillet, remove and set aside.

3. In the same pan, melt butter, whisk in flour, cook 1-2 mins.

4. Slowly add beef broth and cream, whisk until thickened. Add Worcestershire sauce.

5. Return meatballs to sauce and simmer 10 mins. Serve with mashed potatoes or noodles.

Butter Garlic Beef Ribs

Ingredients:

- 3 lbs beef ribs
- Salt and pepper
- 4 tbsp butter
- 6 cloves garlic, minced
- Fresh parsley, chopped

Instructions:

1. Season ribs with salt and pepper. Slow cook or braise at 300°F (150°C) for 3-4 hours until tender.
2. Melt butter, sauté garlic until fragrant.
3. Brush ribs with garlic butter and broil or grill briefly for caramelization.
4. Garnish with parsley and serve.

Cuban Mojo Marinated Steak

Ingredients:

- 2 lbs flank or skirt steak
- Juice of 3 oranges
- Juice of 2 limes
- 6 garlic cloves, minced
- 1/4 cup olive oil
- 1 tsp cumin
- 1 tsp oregano
- Salt and pepper

Instructions:

1. Combine all marinade ingredients. Marinate steak at least 2 hours, preferably overnight.
2. Grill steak on high heat 4-5 mins per side for medium rare.
3. Let rest, slice thinly against the grain, and serve.

www.ingramcontent.com/pod-product-compliance
Lightning Source LLC
LaVergne TN
LVHW081322060526
838201LV00055B/2411